Forever Love

Embracing Triumphs, Marriage, Family, and Overcoming Obstacles

DARLENE MARTIN

FOREVER LOVE

Embracing Triumphs, Marriage, Family, and Overcoming Obstacles

© 2024, Darlene Martin

Print ISBN: 979-8-35096-665-7

eBook ISBN: 979-8-35096-666-4

Contents

Synopsis

When you think of marriage and relationships, what comes to mind?

From what I know about it, as I have been married for thirty-four years and was in a prior long-term relationship, there is no such thing as a perfect relationship. People often say to look for that Knight in Shining Armor. In other words, a perfect romantic partner!

Is there any truth to the idea of a perfect relationship? No!

It's really called an imperfect relationship, because we are not perfect people.

Therefore, please allow me to take you on a journey of rain, pain, and sunshine.

We all come with some baggage, so please allow me to authentically enlighten you on this baggage we both brought to our marriage, plus infidelity, accountability, healing, blended family, and how we both fought for our marriage.

It takes two to make a relationship work!

Author's Biography

Introducing—"Embracing imperfections, Triumphs and Obstacles in Relationships".

Author Darlene S. Martin invites readers into a captivating exploration of imperfect relationships, celebrating the triumphs and acknowledging the obstacles that come with them.

This book is a powerful guide for anyone in a relationship or contemplating entering one, offering invaluable insights and lessons gained from the author's own 34 years of marriage.

As you embark on this transformative read, you will witness the author's story of resilience and perseverance, this includes healing from past wounds, carrying emotional baggage, and confronting the devastating impact of infidelity. Prepare to be moved, motivated, and enlightened as you explore the transformation power of embracing imperfections in relationships. This book is a testament to the strength of the human heart and the enduring power of love.

Introduction

THIS BOOK WAS WRITTEN BASED ON our thirty-four years of marriage, which included true love, blended family, pain, and triumphs, but also a lot of sunshine through the years.

My goal is to share our experiences with anyone who may be going through some challenging times in your marriage and/or your relationships. I am here to share with you that trusting our higher power helped us conquer these thirty-four years of an imperfect marriage.

Fighting for our marriage took faith and a lot of prayer to sustain it. This book also speaks about raising our four children, who are all adults now, the baggage that comes with all relationships, healing, infidelity, and more.

Chapter 1:

When We Met

WHEN I MET MY HUSBAND JOHNNY in 1988, he was a breath of fresh air (in my mind at the time). We met at his mom's house, as I was visiting a cousin and dropping off Avon to his mom. Although I had a full-time job, I sold Avon on the side. Johnny asked me if I sold male cologne, and then asked for a book. I thought it was cool, another sale!! However, when I walked outside and headed to my car, I asked my cousin who Johnny was. She began to explain that he was a good man, single, loved kids, and a hard worker. My cousin then proceeded to point to his Nissan truck and Cadillac. Yes, I was interested at this point, because one thing I was not used to was a man with a good job. We were introduced and, when we spoke later, he mentioned that he asked for that Avon book to get my attention. He was thirty-three and I was twenty-six. We both had children; he had a twelve-year-old daughter and I had my two sons, who were four and nine at the time. We are at thirty-five years of marriage as I am finishing up this book. Thanks to my God!! We have endured many years of tests; a lot of testimonies of what it takes to keep and fight for our family and marriage. We are happily married with grown children and twenty grand-children, both boys and girls—a couple of them have gradu-ated from high school and have been accepted into college. We are living in a home we purchased and love, but bought our first home in 1998! We are both retired, and we love traveling and enjoying family. So, get comfortable as I take you on the journey that got us here.

We met on the rebound, as I like to call it. Both of us were fresh out of a relationship. He had been married for eight years, but had already been divorced for approximately five years when we met. I had just left my two oldest children's father a few months before meeting Johnny. Let me tell you, the baggage was real! I didn't know at the time that we were both bruised from childhood issues and from past relationships. Being only twenty-six, I never even thought about the baggage and all that we bring to a relationship, but I learned about this kind of baggage later in life: the hurt, pain, and just our different types of upbringing. My parents divorced when I was twelve or so. He had only met his biological father twice, but his granddad and mom raised him until she married and he gained a stepfather. There were eight boys in Johnny's family, but I only had one sister growing up until my dad remarried and gave us more little sisters and brothers.

Allow me to elaborate on my first serious relationship (my oldest sons' father), Mr. G. I was fifteen and he was seventeen years old when we started dating. I believed this was my first love at the time. However, this was not real love, it was the type of love and lust that we experience when we are young and immature. I got pregnant at sixteen years old with my oldest son, Geno. Wow! Teenage pregnancy is a whole other book in itself. Silly me, I was taking birth control pills, but not consistently. In my young mind, I always thought that I did not want to be bothered with taking this pill every day.

So, boom! I was pregnant with this little boy and had no knowledge of how I would take care of him. What I did know is that I wasn't going to have an abortion. My mother (RIP to my beautiful Mom), she passed in February 2024) she was very disappointed, although she did eventually accept it. My mother was the reason I succeeded, as she made sure I continued my education. Once I had my son, she stayed up with me at night to help with feeding him, show me how to burp him, change him, and so on.

I really do not know what I would have done if not for her having my back! My mother babysat for me as much as she could, but she had her own life and work. Eventually, I had to find a babysitter outside of my family, and it is so hard leaving your child with a stranger. However, I was blessed to find a good one. When I turned seventeen, I was able to move out and got my own apartment because I wanted privacy. Mr. G and I ended up living together and sharing parental responsibilities. We stayed together for years, as we were trying to make things work out. We ended up having our second son, OB, five years later.

As I think back, this would have never happened if I was more mature in my thinking. We didn't have a lot in common when it came to providing for my sons and wanting more out of life. Financially, I was taking care of mostly everything. At the time, I thought things would get better and I wanted my kids to have the same father. This relationship was not good and caused me to take a lot of baggage to my relationship with Johnny, who is my husband now. The arguments and negative language with Mr. G were not good for my children to be around. Eventually I felt it was time to move on, but I always encouraged my sons to have a father-and-son relationship, and they still do to this day.

My dad and mom worked when we were growing up. They were able to move our family out of an apartment to a house that they purchased together. I remember being so excited; we finally had both a front and back yard to play in. We were running on the freshly installed carpet, looking to see the nice backyard. The real excitement is that the neighborhood was cool, and we met plenty of friends. My husband, Johnny, experienced the same when his mom met his stepfather and they were finally able to purchase a home as well.

He shared with me that it felt good to finally be stable, as they had moved around a lot before that.

Johnny had seven other siblings, all boys. He was most excited about being able to stay in the same school area for years, which allowed him to get a good education and go on to college, where he played college football for Utah State.

Chapter 2:

Family Dynamics/ Blended Families

THE FACT THAT JOHNNY CAME from a family of eight boys was a huge difference from my family, which was only two girls. I remember asking Johnny, "Why are you so fixated on not throwing food away?" because I always throw the leftovers out. However, he would save stuff in the refrigerator or freezer. That's a small thing, but it really got on my last nerve!! We just lived different lifestyles;

he still says to this day I was spoiled. It just took some time to get used to and see each other's perspective on this.

Blended families can be a challenge. We had to not only deal with the children but also with each other and the other parents. Our oldest son, Geno, rebelled. He went to the streets and got involved in a gang. I often asked him why as he became an adult, because I blamed myself a lot although we kept him in sports, and he attended church and family gatherings. Johnny and I also worked full-time. When I asked Geno to tell me in his own words why he rebelled, he said, "I felt resentment because another man who was not my father became the authoritarian in my life, and based on the fact that I had no older siblings I chose to search the streets for a role model/older sibling support."

This really hurt, because I thought that keeping him in sports and church would deter him from going to the streets. He also mentioned that it was a choice and he was influenced by other family members and friends. I continued to beat myself up for a while because I was so laser-focused on working and doing good that I had my head in the sand as far as what was going on in the street because I wasn't out there. One thing is that I should have spent more individual time talking to my sons about how they felt. Also, Johnny knew there was something going on, but I thought, *Not my kid!!*

I got caught up in trying to make my husband happy because I figured he was the best thing that had happened to us. Johnny went with me to their activities as well because he loved sports and played football from high school through college.

Although my oldest son and I have talked about this topic briefly in the past, I told him I was writing this book and I wanted his input. This made tears come to my eyes because I already suspected that it was something like this. Unfortunately, parenthood does not come with instructions. Make sure your children feel included and also speak with them about their feelings, because I could have done a better job at that, in hindsight! I have often thought about this, and I told myself that if I could do it all over again it would be different.

However, God didn't say the same, because he put my now-husband Johnny in our life for very good reasons as I look back! This man taught my children how to be men: be responsible, get a good job. He made sure that they knew how to cut grass and fix things. He also displayed to them how to treat a woman well by how he treated me. This all showed up in their adult life for the most part.

When I met Johnny, he said he had been married for approximately eight years but was divorced. My response was, "If you are divorced, I need to see the divorce papers, please." He told me he had to dig them up because they were stored away. I replied, "Well, start digging because this relationship will not go anywhere until I see the papers." He told me that he would find them and get them back to me. I believe it was a couple of days later that he told me that he had found the divorce papers, so we met, and he had the proof. That is funny to me now!

By showing me proof that he was divorced, I felt that we could continue to pursue the relationship because this showed me that he wanted it too, and I wasn't going to deal with a man who was still married. Our first date was at my apartment. I invited him over for breakfast because that was my favorite meal of the day. I served eggs, bacon, grits, and biscuits smothered in strawberries. Yes, he loved my cooking.

I must say, when he arrived before breakfast, he called from the intercom because I lived in a gated community. At first, I got cold feet because I was just coming out of the relationship with my ex and really was not ready for a new one. Therefore, my first thought was not to let him in. However, Johnny was very charming on that intercom and talked me into letting him in. The conversation was great as we sat on the balcony of my apartment. I admired his educational background, his intellect, his hard work, his independence, and his pleasant personality.

One thing about when we first met made me laugh! I did not like his hair; this was back in the eighties, so people were still wearing Afros. I didn't really mind that, but his was wack! I was telling this to a friend, and her response was, "So, are you going to let hair stop you from potentially having a good man"? That can be changed!" And it was. I talked him into the jerry curl. That suited him a lot better, in my opinion.

At the time, my mindset was my man had to be good looking and all that stuff that doesn't really matter. Being twenty-six speaks to that. That same thing brought a bunch of disappointments in my life. When I was a teenager and met my ex, I was just looking at his looks!

That's not what we should seek in a relationship. However, I feel like they need to be attractive in some type of way. The man God has for you may not be the man you dream of or envision him to be!

Chapter 3:

Disciplining our Children

I KIND OF REGRET THIS, BUT I WOULD not let Johnny, discipline my sons from my prior relationship. My mom used to tell me, do not put a man before your children. So, in my young mind, I figured, *Okay, you cannot tell them what to do, leave that to me, and you definitely cannot spank them.* However, Johnny felt some type of way about this. Especially when my oldest, Geno, started showing signs of disobedience by hanging out with peers he should not have, which led him to gangs. My head was in the sand, I guess, because neither of us lived this life, so I didn't see the red flags!

Johnny did, though, but in hindsight, I know now that I was over-protecting them because I already felt bad about their biological father not being there with them anymore. Therefore, instead of looking at my husband as a father, I treated him like my boyfriend. We actually were together for a year and a half before he proposed to me. You see, coming out of a bad relationship, I brought so much baggage into this marriage. I was hurt by my ex, so I didn't trust Johnny right away! I remember he always made this statement, "I am not him!" Well, it took me a while to trust him because I had put a wall up no matter what he said.

Although Johnny tried to show me how to raise boys, I wasn't actually internalizing this message and I did not grow up with any brothers, only one sister. One thing I learned later was that he didn't really have experience with raising boys either. However, he was raised with seven brothers by his stepdad and grandfather. There is not one blueprint for raising anyone, and our parents and grandparents did not always get it right either. But on some basic matters, he knew more than I did, of course, about raising a boy to be a man.

Our oldest son, Geno, ultimately ended up going to juvenile detention and then prison. As I stated earlier, he rebelled because he was not feeling the situation that I brought a stepfather into his life. However, he did share with me that it was also his choice. I was devastated when he went to prison. I blamed myself and my husband, but as I think back, I never really blamed his biological father because I had kind of blocked him out of my mind. It would have been too much for me to dwell on him also. Johnny and I did not leave Geno's side when he had to do that prison time, because we still had hope that if we stuck by him, he would have the chance to change. Therefore, we sent boxes and money and visited him often. Well, I actually did most of the visiting, but Johnny backed me up on everything. It paid off because when he got out, he turned things around: he went to a business college, a truck driving school, and got his class-A license, and he attained his GED while incarcerated; he now also owns his own clothing line business and is an awesome father to his two boys! He is also working on an additional business as we speak. Geno has not been incarcerated at this point for approximately eighteen years!!! The reason I am speaking about my oldest often is because he kind of set the foundation for his brother (OB), who is five years younger than him.

OB started following in his footsteps as well; incarceration, repeat! Geno inadvertently influenced him to feel the same way about Johnny. However, the same thing happened for him; we stuck by him, too, and now he is also doing very well, working and raising his children, and has been out for approximately ten years. OB also has goals to start his own business soon.

Now, this is something I would like to note: we had Johnny Jr. (Johnny's and my biological son together), and as I think back on this, both Geno and OB always talked to him to try and keep him from going the route they went. He got into some trouble, but not like them. However, the concern is that Johnny Sr. seemed to treat him a little differently than my other two, who are his stepsons. I accused him of that, but I don't feel like he even realized it. Johnny Jr. is his only biological son, because his only other biological child is my stepdaughter. Johnny Jr. is a well known Chef now and has been for years. He graduated from Le Cordon Bleu Culinary

Arts school. Johnny Jr. also has several children and is taking care of them. I am very proud of ALL of our adult children, and how they have overcome obstacles. My stepdaughter Nisha is also doing well and is working as a Nurse and taking care of her children.

My stepdaughter and my relationship grew to be fine, but I feel like it could have been better if it was not for one of her family members putting negativity in her head, but I digress.

In hindsight, I wonder if I were to let him discipline my boys more, would that have helped or made it worse? Well, that is one of those unknown thoughts that I had to let go of because, like a therapist shared with me, how would you know? We both did the best that we knew how, because we didn't have instructions for parenting; nobody does. The thing about life is we all live and learn from our mistakes. We are both believers, so we do know how to pray and trust God even though we could not even see our way at the time. We have walked by faith and not by sight for a very, very long time.

Chapter 4:

Communication and Compromise

OUR FAMILY TRIES TO UNDERSTAND each other's personalities and communication styles. For example, one member may prefer to express their feelings through writing while another may prefer to talk things out face-to-face. By recognizing and respecting these differences, our family worked on communicating effectively, which helped avoid misunderstandings.

Another aspect of communication and compromise is acknowledging the different family dynamics within a blended family. It is important to recognize that each member brings their own experiences and expectations from their previous family dynamic. This may include different parenting styles, household rules, and traditions.

We found it important to acknowledge and respect these differences while working together. For example, we both worked full-time, therefore we had to discuss different ways and times to communicate. We leave notes to each other about tasks and ideas. Our family worked together to establish new roles and responsibilities that would work for everyone, ensuring that everyone felt valued and included.

It is also important to remember that communication and compromise are ongoing processes. As the family grows and changes over time, so do the dynamics and expectations within the family. It is essential to regularly check in with each other, hold family meetings, and adjust rules and guidelines as needed.

Regular check-ins are especially important during transitions, such as when a new member joins the family, when the family moves to a new home, or when there are unforeseen issues to discuss. These check-ins provide a space for everyone to express their concerns and feelings, work together to find solutions, and ensure everyone feels heard and valued.

In conclusion, building a successful blended family requires open and honest communication and a willingness to compromise. By establishing family rules and guidelines together, respecting each other's differences, and regularly checking in with each other, families can work together to build a strong and cohesive family unit. While it may not always be easy, the rewards of a successful blended family are immeasurable, providing a loving and supportive environment for all members to thrive.

Blending two families together can be difficult and overwhelming. It requires patience, understanding, and a willingness to compromise. We will explore the importance of communication and compromise and the challenges of merging two families.

Building a successful blended family is not an easy feat, as it involves a lot of changes, adaptations, and compromises. We have experienced the trials and tribulations that come with blending two families, but through our reflections and experiences, we have learned what it takes to build a successful blended family.

Our family found that communication and compromise were essential to building our blended family successfully. We established a set of rules and guidelines that everyone agreed to, which helped to minimize conflicts and misunderstandings. We held regular family meetings to discuss any issues and work together to find solutions. Bringing two families together successfully when children are involved is challenging, because the children may struggle with accepting new family members and adjusting to changes. Another significant challenge was dealing with the expectations and reactions of extended family members. Some family members were supportive, while others were not. It was crucial for Johnny and I to stay true to ourselves and our family's needs and not be swayed by others' opinions,

Chapter 5:

Maintaining the Fire of Romance

SOMETIMES COUPLES OUTGROW each other or perhaps find other interests that they may like in general. We must try to take an interest in at least one thing our partner loves to do. For instance, we had a lot of things in common, but one thing I wasn't used to doing was fishing. That's one of his sports so I took interest in it because he would always ask me to go. I'm happy I did because although I wasn't so much into fishing, I found it very relaxing being by the water.

We even eventually bought a boat which I never thought I would get on one but now I love to cruise. Till this day I still will not bait the pole or touch the fish but he does it for me! One thing for sure is we now spend a lot of time together being on the water. Had I not taken an interest, I wouldn't even know that I love being out on the water so much. I incorporate bringing my book or magazines, I have a little wine and just chill. When we met I shared with him how I loved to dance. Fortunately he does too, but not as much as I do. We would always go out dancing because he took interest in what I loved to do. Even until this day we continue to indulge in what we both love to do.

Love languages; our love language can be very different, therefore you may miss the mark of your mate trying to display the signs or show you love. Most women were taught that the flowers, chocolates and jewelry gifts were what should be given. However, don't forget about you may be shown love in different ways. Johnny loves to plant and pick flowers out of the yard for me. That had to grow on me because I was going with what people always said the norm was. As soon as I learned about various love languages, I really appreciated him more. In a relationship you must find what works for the both of you and not what everyone else is doing. Especially on social media because you will be surprised that some of that stuff is just for show.

Finally, we must communicate to our partner what we like as well because nobody is a mind reader and also, giving hints doesn't always work. Please appreciate the effort that the person put in because it's the thought that counts.

Chapter 6:

Success of our Blended Family

A S I REFLECT ON THE SUCCESS OF my blended family, I am filled with gratitude and accomplishment. We have overcome so many challenges and come out stronger and more united because of them.

One of the most memorable aspects of our success has been the vacations and trips we have taken together. These trips have allowed us to bond and create lasting memories as a family. These trips include beach vacations, fishing trips, and camping, just to name a few. We have explored new places and experienced new adventures together. Through these trips, we have learned more about each other and have grown closer as a family.

However, success in a blended family is not just about fun vacations. It is also about the day-to-day routines and interactions that make up family life. As our family has grown and changed over time, we have had to adapt and evolve together. This is another important aspect of success in blended families: Recognizing that change is inevitable and being open to embracing it together.

Another key aspect of our success has been our commitment to supporting and loving each other. We have faced many challenges as a blended family, but through it all, we have remained united in our love for each other. This has allowed us to overcome even the most difficult obstacles and strengthened our family bond.

As I look back on our journey as a blended family, I am proud of all that we have accomplished together and I am excited for all that the future holds.

When Johnny and I decided to blend our families, we knew we had to approach it with patience and understanding. It was essential to give the children time and space to process their feelings and emotions. It wasn't easy for them to accept new family members and adjust to changes in their family dynamic. We had to be there for them, listen to them, and make sure they felt heard and valued. Now that we have grandchildren, we will exhibit and repeat what we have learned, although they are a different type of generation!

Co-parenting with our ex-partners was another challenge we had to navigate. It required communication, compromise, and mutual respect. We had to find ways to work together and ensure that the children's needs were being met. It wasn't always easy, but we knew it was essential to maintain a healthy co-parenting relationship for the children's sake.

Despite—and maybe because of—our challenges, our blended family has grown and changed over time. We have become a strong, supportive, and loving family unit. We have continued traditions, such as family gatherings. However, our children are adults now, so they plan most of their own trips with their families and my grandchildren often as well. We have built strong relationships with one another. It has been a journey, and we have learned a lot along the way.

One of the most important things we learned is that change is inevitable in a blended family. It is essential to be open to adapting and evolving together. As our family grew and changed, we had to find new ways to communicate and compromise. We had to find new ways to create a sense of belonging and ownership for every family member.

In conclusion, building a blended family comes with its challenges and changes. It requires patience, understanding, and a willingness to communicate and compromise. It is important to give the children time and space to process their emotions, co-parent with mutual respect, and stay true to the family's needs. Despite the challenges, a blended family can be a strong, supportive, and loving family unit that creates new traditions and builds strong relationships.

Chapter 7:

Love and Support

I CAN ATTEST THAT LOVE AND SUP-
port are essential in building a successful blended family. Our family has faced many challenges over the years, from adjusting to new family members to co-parenting with ex-partners. Through it all, our love and support for one another have helped us navigate these difficulties and come out stronger on the other side.

We show our love and support for each other by creating a safe and comfortable home environment. We make sure to have regular family dinners and game nights where we can bond and connect with one another. We also make it a priority to acknowledge and celebrate each other's achievements, big or small. This helps to build a sense of belonging and connection within our blended family.

It is also important to support each other through difficult times. Whether it's helping a stepchild through a tough time at school or being there for a spouse during a stressful work period, we make sure to be there for each other. We offer a listening ear, a shoulder to cry on, and words of encouragement.

Of course, love and support aren't just about day-to-day interactions. They're also about the big moments, such as weddings and graduations. Our family comes together to celebrate these milestones and show our love and support for each other. We also make sure to include all family members, including children from previous relationships and extended family members.

Overall, the love and support within our blended family have been instrumental in our success. It has allowed us to work through challenges, build strong relationships, and create a loving and supportive home environment.

Blending two families is not an easy feat, but it can be achieved with determination and perseverance. As discussed in this chapter, communication, compromise, love, and support are crucial elements in building a successful blended family. Our experiences and reflections serve as a guide for families who are embarking on their own journey of blending two families together.

Chapter 8:

Healing

S O, THEN THE LONG AND HARD WORK begins: Huge sigh! Counseling and therapy began. We both learned a lot about ourselves, and for the most part, I learned so much more about him because good counselors will bring it out. He was reluctant at first, and did not share as much as I did. You see, we not only bring baggage from prior relationships but also from our childhood trauma that people only address later in adult life and many will never address. We must address our traumas and own them to start the healing process, or we will just continue to hurt ourselves and others around us.

The therapy, for the most part, was simply to help us begin communicating effectively. He was interpreting almost everything I said differently than what I meant and what I thought I was saying. I, at times, did, too, because of how he wasn't communicating what he really wanted to say. Our counselors, who were a male and female together, taught us ink-pen therapy. Basically, when I was talking, I had the pen, and he could not say anything until I gave him the pen. At this point, it was his turn to speak and tell me what he thought I said and vice versa. To be honest, he got often misinterpreted what he thought I said. Can you imagine? An entire conversation and not getting through what you are trying to say! Everyone is on different levels when it comes to communicating.

One thing Johnny also did was hear me, but not really listen for understanding. I'm trying to tell you that until communication becomes effective and you understand each other, it will be an uphill battle. Sometimes, you might be good at communication but have other issues, and either way it's a good idea to lay those issues to rest by sharing your feelings with each other.

Our counselors also addressed the infidelity; Although these particular counselors were not the only ones we counseled with for this topic. After sharing with them our story—and we had already been together for some years before this happened—they thought that we should work our issues out by talking and opening up more about what we want for ourselves as far as intimacy. We both had a hard time back then speaking the truth about what we wanted. Although we didn't really have any problems with our sex life, Johnny felt a need to step outside of our marriage and cheat, therefore based on that it was very hard to understand at that time. You see, sex isn't everything in a marriage. Men need to feel wanted, needed, peaceful, and loved, just like women. I actually did not know this at the time. I always thought it was all about the women and our needs.

I feel like some of the time when a man cheats, it's not the sex!!! In fact, what I learned is that some will step out on you to get that peace and the love that they are missing at home. I mean, we were both broken from past relationships, not to mention the childhood issues that almost everyone carries with them into other relationships. Part of this healing journey is that we must get some help so that we may see ourselves for who we really are!! Both parties have to be willing to do this.

I remember blaming him for the infidelity because I thought, *OMG nothing is worse than betrayal.* The lying when you were coming home and stating that you were someplace else. Pretending that our love life was intact, showing me love, but at the same time being out with another woman. So in my mind I was like, *Nah! Although I treated you meanly at times, I didn't let you touch my kids to discipline them, and I also demeaned your character; this was all because I was still in the mode from my prior relationship's trauma, that did not make me worthy of you being fully committed to me.* This right here, folks, was a very hard pill for me to swallow!

When I hear people talk about cheating, as most people call it, it seems that most women say it's a deal breaker, but depending on the circumstances, it should not be. If you are in love, have a lot in common, and this man has a whole lot to offer besides cheating, it is worth evaluating the circumstances and getting some therapy and counseling. We fought for our marriage because we had seen so much more and knew that somehow and for some reason God put us together to be soulmates. The most important part is that both parties have to want the marriage to work! But remember, Physical abuse should NOT be tolerated at any time.

Healing is definitely an ongoing process, and I continue to get therapy today. We can always become a better version of ourselves, and it's continuous!!

As I stated in an earlier chapter, Johnny went in front of an entire church to admit he wasn't faithful and wanted to ask for my forgiveness. This was therapy for both of us. When I heard that, it made me feel some accountability from him as well as soothed and comforted me in knowing that he was remorseful about what he had done. Accountability, as I mentioned above, is also a good sign that the other person wants it to work out and is willing to work on the marriage. It takes two, period!! One thing about most men: If they want you, they will definitely change for you. It is just that simple.

Chapter 9:

The Baggage

O BVIOUSLY, WHEN GROWN PEOPLE get together and attempt to build a relationship, both bring along some baggage. This stems from childhood issues, how you were raised, personality traits, prior relationships, and so on. My goodness, where should I start?

When I met Johnny, what I first noticed was . . . how he spoke and that he had a good job and a nice truck and car. I was like *Woooooowwwww*! And he loved children. He did have a daughter, but told me he was working on a relationship with her because he could not see her. I must say that I encouraged him not to ever give up on her because he had a right to see her.

We spoke about my boys, too, and he mentioned all the things he would bring to the table; because he had played football in high school, junior college, and at Utah State College, he would put my two oldest into sports. He would also take them places like to play in the snow and so forth. Yeah, he was selling himself very well.

One thing I would do differently is not move so fast. I met him just as I had come out of a toxic relationship about six month earlier. That didn't give me much time to spend with my boys alone. I brought this man, the only man other than their father, into my life. I would not advise anyone to do that. Take time with your children alone first.

As we started going on more dates, feelings became deeper between the two of us. He introduced me to his mother, but he had only met his father once. [Side note: get to know that person's family and history before getting married. It can tell you a whole lot about that person.

During the dating period, Johnny started sharing his hobbies with me. He loved fishing, because that was something his whole family did, basically. Therefore, we went on a fishing date. I had some exposure to fishing, because my parents took us there a few times, although we were little girls. I don't remember actually fishing, though. One thing about it: I love sitting by the water because it was so relaxing. He taught me how to throw the hook out and reel in, because I didn't like baiting that hook.

The funny thing is, I was trying to be cute that day, but I wore the wrong shoes. I was walking down some rocks to get to the water, and almost fell. Johnny caught me because he didn't get too far ahead, because he already knew I was nervous. He gained lots of points because I felt protected.

I didn't really have too many hobbies, just taking care of my children, but I loved to dance, so he took me out to clubs sometimes. One other things is that we both were believers, so our faith kept us strong, as we started going to church together and taking the kids with us. One thing our parents had in common is we were raised in the church. That part has paid off big time.

As we continued to date, have fun, and get to know each other and my boys, plus the rest of our families, Johnny proposed to me in a jewelry store. We had both hinted around that we wanted to be married one day. I still have that picture when he got down on his knees. I said, "Yes," and this was approximately a little more than a year after we started dating. I remember vividly the day he got on his knees in a jewelry store.

After that, the ring and all, we started looking at dates and people we wanted to have in our wedding. As we were planning, I picked out the colors, wedding party members, and so on. Then, Boom! like eight weeks or so into the planning, I started feeling sick. My mind went straight to pregnancy because I already had two signs, so I knew the signs. But I was thinking in the back of my head, *Nooooo!* Johnny had told me he could not have any more children. His daughter from his first marriage was twelve, and he had tried to have another child with a prior relationship, and he could not. Little old naive me at twenty-six figured *Okay, then, I will take myself off the birth control pill.* I really did not like the pill, because research had showed that it could cause cancer. I also said I did not want any more children. In hindsight, I think about how naïve I was. My pregnancy was awful, in the sense that the morning sickness lasted for five months (more than half of my pregnancy!).

Johnny had never really gone through morning sickness like I was having during this pregnancy. He got so concerned and upset. I tried to tell him I had experienced the same thing with my boys and it was normal for me. Johnny was so very happy when we found out it was a boy. I think I went into a sort of depression for a bit, but he always reassured me that he would be there for me, our biological son together and my other two. We also made sure that his daughter from his previous marriage was part of the family, too.

So, back to the planned wedding. We cancelled it, mainly because I was so sick. The morning sickness took so much energy away form my body. This meant having to contact the people we had already notified and asked to be in the wedding party. I felt terrible, because the dresses were in the process of being made. The colors were going to be red and white; a white lace and red satin combination that was just beautiful.

Long story short, we ended up going to Reno, where a lot of people went to get married. We picked out a dress and his suit and the bouquet of flowers. We took our witnesses and other family members. Yes, we got married while pregnant and I was showing my baby bump. The greatest part about it is that we had family there, and our honeymoon suite was amazing, with a huge hot tub that we both relaxed in after the wedding. I used to regret that I never had my wedding, but the marriage is all that counts anyway because there would be work ahead.

Before I gave birth to my third son, who was named after Johnny, he suggested that we move into a house because our family was growing. It was such a blessing to get out of that little apartment. We found our first home and rented it. Then the day came that I gave birth to Johnny Jr. He looked just like his father, Johnny Sr. The house was perfect for our children, but let me tell you, this was the beginning of some things to come: the work of being a mother of three, working parent, and a wife began. We were still trying to figure this marriage and blended family thing out as well.

Surviving a Broken Heart

When trust has been an issue in any form or fashion, it's a daily continuous work in progress for both people. I must say that if I wasn't a believer and prayer warrior, we would have been divorced a long time ago! It's been thirty-five years now when I am writing this book. He is a believer as well, so God kept showing us that we must fight!! I know now that this was God's plan, and this book is absolutely being written because it is my purpose and assignment. Yes, my flesh was fighting his will a lot, but the Holy Spirit kept bringing me back . . . you know, that little voice that quietly comes to our mind and speaks.

Johnny held himself accountable in many ways. One of them was that he met me at a church we had been attending, but I had told him I was going alone because I needed some time to think and speak with God. However, he showed up there anyway. It wasn't the regular church services; it was an evening program. He asked to meet me at church so that we could both pray, and that little voice I was talking about in my head said, *Let him come!* When he got there, he was seated next to me as I was asking God . . . *Now I know you sent him here for a reason, but I am not feeling this.*

We sat and enjoyed the service, and then I believe the pastor opened up for prayer or something, so my hubby stood up and went up there. I was thinking, *Okay, he is going up for prayer, cool,* but as he got up there, he said he needed to say something first. He apologized to me in front of the entire church and asked for forgiveness for his infidelity. Now keep in mind he does not usually admit anything in front of a bunch of people. Anyway, tears just started coming from everywhere to the point that I started getting choked up.

So, I had my answer from God that this is why I should have let him come. Sometimes we have to be obedient and just walk by faith. That meant the world to me, because when he showed himself accountable like this, it showed remorse, which meant he was serious about doing what it took to save our marriage. This is true for anyone in this situation. If they are willing to hold themselves accountable, they are serious about working to save the relationship. I thought back to something I had read in the bible about renewing his strength, so I put two plus two together.

As I mentioned earlier in the book, when coming together in a relationship, we both bring baggage, but how will we know if we do not at least help each other unpack that luggage? I am not saying this is for all situations, because you should never stay in a physically or mentally abusive relationship!!!!!! However, it does take putting in the work, especially if you want it to last forever! I can't say my forever is here yet, but thirty-five years sure seems like it!

Forgiveness and Brain Encounters

The hardest part for me was having to work through all the thoughts that popped up in my head often: revisiting the affair, how and when it happened, why it happened, and often retaliation.

Why didn't I cheat back in order to make him feel the same way? That was an easy answer: I have too much respect for myself and I knew that this isn't what God would have me do. Besides, if I was going to work to save my marriage, why add more damage to it? He is the one that has to answer to God, not me. I did have emotional outbursts because my mind just would not let it go. As I continue to speak with a therapist and read self-help books, the conclusion is: That's just how the mind works. However, I did learn that the best way to fight off reappearing thoughts is to dismiss them as soon as they come to your mind.

Chapter 10:

Infidelity

ALLOW ME TO TAKE YOU ON A LIT-
tle journey that led up to infidelity.

After moving into our first home, we enjoyed the space because it gave our boys space as well. I remember having Johnny's fortieth birthday party there. We were so happy to invite family over to our lovely, spacious home that we were blessed to rent. Johnny Jr was around a year and a half years old when we moved there. Geno and OB were nine and four and going to elementary school. The school was right around the corner, which was so convenient. However, we were both still dealing with baggage. As I mentioned earlier, since we both had children from prior relationships and had to deal with our co-parents, I can honestly say my baggage was more recent and deeper than his. Or so I thought. My relationship with the older boys' father was basically a lot of chaos. We were both really young when we got together; I was fifteen and he was seventeen. When Geno was born, I was sixteen, and five years later we had another one because I thought I wanted to stay with and marry the man I had children with. Although my parents divorced when I was approximately twelve, I thought I wanted to do it the right way. This was not the right idea. Never stay with a person just because you have children together. We argued all of the time; there was some verbal abuse, and some physical abuse on my part.

So, now let's get into how I found out about the infidelity. The suspicion was always there because of the baggage from my prior relationship—therefore, I didn't trust men in general, and it showed. One morning I had a gut feeling something was going on because Johnny worked shift work (day shift, swing shift, and graveyard), changing each week. On this particular day, he was on the graveyard shift, from 11 p.m. to 6 a.m. I worked the day shift, so I set the alarm for 7 a.m. to get up for work, but he wasn't home yet the way he usually was.

I started calling, but there was no answer after several calls. This was unusual, because he always answered my calls. At this point, my gut feeling was that he was out with another woman. Johnny arrived home approximately an hour later. This meant to me that he had not been at work.

I had already decided I was calling off work because I needed some answers! As soon as he walked in, of course, the questions started about his whereabouts. He was shocked that I was there, because he expected me to be on my way to work. When I approached Johnny, he started lying about where he had been. However, I quickly shut the lies down by telling him he had better start speaking the truth quickly because this was the only opportunity he would have before things got really ugly!! As he started to see how serious I was, he then said, "Let me take a shower, and we will talk after. This was a red flag.

So, he got into the shower and while he was in there, I checked his shirt because it appeared to have makeup on it, and it did! That was all the evidence that I needed. I was pretty angry, but still trying to hold my composure because horrible thoughts were going through my mind. Once he got out of the shower and I showed him the makeup, he knew it was best if he started spilling the beans. Johnny started to tell me how I had been treating him like less than a partner in our marriage, with name-calling, arguments, and not letting him have any say in disciplining the boys. So, he stepped outside of our marriage and cheated. He stated he was trying to find some peace and was questioning our relationship. As we continued to talk, I explained to him that was the worst thing he could do in a marriage because I probably would never trust him again.

At this point he agreed that he had made a mistake, apologized, and asked if we could please try and work on our marriage. My response was, "Who is she?" and he stated that it was not anyone that I knew, it was just one night, and things didn't work out anyway.

My response was, well, the expression on his face was unforgettable!! I told him that if it wasn't serious and was a one-night stand, then I needed to verify that with her, so take me to her! He finally agreed after trying to get out of taking me. When we arrived, I got out of the car first because I had questions, I wanted to see what she looked like and confirm what he said. He took me to the restaurant that she worked at because she worked for her aunt's business, and he knew she would be there on the morning shift.

Once we got in, I asked which one she was. They both were surprised to see us, according to the looks on their faces. I introduced myself as Johnny's wife and said, "Johnny just confessed to me that you two had a one-night stand, and said the relationship was not going to continue, so can you please confirm what is going on?"

She started explaining that nothing was serious and he was correct about the one-night stand, however she said that they did meet a couple of times in the restaurant. She also stated that she wasn't into him like that and did not plan on seeing him anymore and, furthermore, he told me he was separated. I let her know that wasn't true! She continued to assure me that the relationship would not be going any further. This all added up, because as we were driving there, I purposely asked him questions so I could compare what he said before we arrived with what she told me, and everything pretty much added up.

Although the work continues of healing from this and trusting again, this was a good start because this was accountability on his part. At that point, we started doing the work to help us get through all of this. We sought counseling from a variety of people, which totally helped us. Cheating is not a deal breaker in my opinion. It's a decision that everyone needs to make for themselves. It's quite disturbing to me when I hear so many people say that if he cheats, that is it! You have to ask yourself first, Is your relationship worth fighting for? What are the pros and cons? Do I love this person? Do we both want it to work? Most importantly, take a look at your faults and not just the other person's faults!! People do not want to do the hard work, and I know it can be very challenging! So, to each its own.

Chapter 11:

Intimacy and Sex after Cheating

WELL, WELL, WELL! THIS IS VERY challenging, because just the thought of him touching me and knowing he had been with someone else was devastating for me. All I could think of was, *How could he come home to me after sex with someone else (the betrayal of it all)!* Therefore, I withheld sex for a couple of months. All sorts of thoughts were going through my head because I wondered, *What if he goes out again and cheats?* I really did not care at that point, because that would have shown me that he did not care about our relationship.

Instead, he decided to go along on this journey with me and hold himself accountable by understanding why I did not want this type of interaction and that I was healing. Of course, my mind was always all over the place: Will he do it again? Was the culprit in my mind! What was it like with her? Was I not attractive enough? You name it. I made it all about me. However, what I figured out through counseling, and so on is that it was not just about me! It is also about him . . . .some men get exposed to seeing other men cheat in their family as they were growing up. Others may have had a mother who slept around and they were exposed to it. You see, children learn from what they see when growing up, not what you say.

Another factor is that sex can be an addiction for some as well. Many factors play into this, and that is one reason it is very important to get to know him and his family history before marriage. So, the big question now is, do you both love each other enough to get counseling and unpack it all? If yes, there is a lot of work that will have to take place! Therefore, just like a flower to become healthy and beautiful, it needs plenty of water, sunshine, and plant food to grow.

It is the same for a relationship. Sex is not the only thing that matters to a man . . . read that sentence again! He needs love, affection, peace, and honesty to be treated well, just like women need. Often, women do not see it the same way because it is all about us. Therefore, as I stated earlier in this book, I brought baggage from my prior relationship that caused me to treat him badly. He tried to talk to me about how I made him feel, but I just ignored him. One thing about infidelity, it does not start with sex; it starts with those conversations they might have at work or someplace with other women about the marriage/relationship problems. Then the sex comes because one of them takes it there.

To sum this up, the cheater must be willing and understanding about how stepping out and having an affair with someone else made you feel. You must talk about it! You must both attend counseling so that both get a clear understanding from a third party, someone that neither of you knows so that it's not one-sided. This type of work takes time, faith, patience, and a lot of love.

Let It Go

Let go of everything that will get in the way of saving your marriage, including:

- Baggage

- Grudges

- Anger

- Blame

- Shame

- Negative thoughts

Some of the reasons I feel my husband is my soulmate include:

- He encourages me in all endeavors I set out to do myself.

- He loves me without doubt.

- He supports me; even if he can't see the end, he trusts me.

- He does not try to change the person I am, but he communicates that he has.

- His love language is unique to the way I need to be loved.

A man who changes his ways just for you is real love.

Chapter 12:

The Mask, Makeup, and Smiles

I REMEMBER WHEN I WAS GOING through it all and trying to stay focused, but pretending everything was all right. I kept that fake smile up, but was hurting inside.

One morning, I went to work, trying to look as if everything was normal. I usually wear a little makeup sometimes, but this was a bit different because I piled it on like I was really painting the hurt out of my soul! A bit deep, ha? Psychologically, I didn't even know at the time, but in my mind, I was covering up all the hurt and pain that I was going through.

I believed that looking good on the outside would make me feel better on the inside, but that is obviously an illusion and a temporary fix. Until I reached out to a therapist, I didn't even understand it all, but I just knew it made me feel a little better. However, I was pushing away that hurt and pain to a huge level of stress. When we do not allow ourselves to release stress, I believe it filters through our bodies and causes internal illness.

I remember going in to work one day and a co-worker literally told me that I looked better without makeup! Kind of funny, right? In hindsight, I figured out that it was my higher power telling me, "Look, take that makeup off and get to the root of the problem." Sometimes we don't want to get to the root of the problem because it takes a lot of work, but we have to.

I was trying to be a mother, but my children were going in a totally different direction than what I instilled in them;

working as a mother and trying to work on my marriage had taken a toll on me. Never mind my own personal issues . . . Geeeeesh!

It is amazing how our life experiences become our testimony, and God wants us to use them for his purpose to bless others. I hope more people will do this, because some feel ashamed of their experiences and do not know we go through all this stuff for a reason and to help people who are going through the same thing.

A strong marriage or relationship requires two people who choose to love each other even when they struggle to like each other. Don't replace him. Teach him to be the man you want. You will never find a perfect man, but you can build him up to be your perfect man. A good man seeks peace. His priority is not just beauty or sex, but peace also.